FOUR LAST THINGS

T0348013

Lisa Tierney-Keogh

FOUR LAST THINGS

OBERON BOOKS
LONDON

WWW.OBERONBOOKS.COM

First published in 2019 by Oberon Books Ltd
521 Caledonian Road, London N7 9RH
Tel: +44 (0) 20 7607 3637 / Fax: +44 (0) 20 7607 3629
e-mail: info@oberonbooks.com
www.oberonbooks.com

Copyright © Lisa Tierney-Keogh, 2009

Lisa Tierney-Keogh is hereby identified as author of this play in accordance
with section 77 of the Copyright, Designs and Patents
Act 1988. The author has asserted her moral rights.

All rights whatsoever in this play are strictly reserved and application
for performance etc. should be made before rehearsal to Alex Rusher at
Independent Talent, 40 Whitfield St, Bloomsbury, London W1T 2RH .
No performance may be given unless a licence has been obtained, and
no alterations may be made in the title or the text of the play without the
author's prior written consent.

You may not copy, store, distribute, transmit, reproduce or otherwise make
available this publication (or any part of it) in any form, or binding or by
any means (print, electronic, digital, optical, mechanical, photocopying,
recording or otherwise), without the prior written permission of the
publisher.

A catalogue record for this book is available from the British Library.

PB ISBN: 9781786828125
E ISBN: 9781786828132

Cover photography of Young woman standing in snow by Thomas Northcut

eBook conversion by Lapiz Digital Services, India.

Visit www.oberonbooks.com to read more about all our books and to buy them. You will
also find features, author interviews and news of any author events, and you can sign up for
e-newsletters and be the first to hear about our new releases.

10 9 8 7 6 5 4 3 2 1

For J.

Four Last Things was first performed on 14 September 2009 as part of the 2009 Absolut Dublin Fringe Festival with the following cast:

BRENDAN	Eamonn Hunt
JANE	Jane McGrath
BOB	Moe Dunford

Production Team

Director	Garrett Keogh
Producer	Lisa Tierney-Keogh
Designer	Conleth White
Designer	Marie Tierney

Four Last Things was produced in Dublin in 2009, New York in 2014, Mexico City in 2015, Portland in 2019.

Characters

JANE, early twenties.

BRENDAN, her father, late fifties/early sixties.

BOB, the farm dog.

The play is set in the present on a rural farm
in the midlands of Ireland.

A man, his daughter, and her dog enter and take their places onstage.

JANE *(A Sunday Night.)*: The beech trees in the
yard on our farm are tall. So big they
sometimes feel like they block out the
sky above them. I can stand, and listen to
them, talking in the wind. The crows act
like they own them. Swaying backwards
and forwards, on waves of bark, cawing
at me. They chitter chatter at me. But I've
no interest in listening to them. They're
only old crows, full of gossip and slander
and dirt. *(Imitates.)* "Would you look at
the state of her hair." "I know, she's really
after letting herself go." *(Pause.)* There's
a clean feeling in the air. Even when my
brother, Tim, spreads slurry, there's still
a sense of freshness to this countryside. I
can see that *(Pause.)* It's the *silence* that gets
me. The nothingness of every, dragging,
day punctuated by the odd visit from a vet,
a passing car far down on the main road
below, or, if you're really lucky, a couple
of Jehovah's Witnesses might venture their
way up to the house... "We'd like to talk
to you about Jesus." "Great. I'll put the
kettle on." *(Pause.)* It's this solitude, this
quiet, that *they* seem to love so much, that
fills me with dread. Standing in our dusty

1

yard on this most lonely Sunday night, I want to take the trees and swap them for the buildings of Dublin city. Swap that big beech tree by the hay barn for Liberty Hall. Change that cluster over there for the heights the docks are stretching to. Swap dust and hay for concrete and litter. The tiny, dribbling stream in the back field for the murky waters of the Liffey. The smell of grass for the smell of hops, wafting downriver from Guinnesses. The cows in the fields for people, crossing on a red light on Dame Street. Swap the tractors for tour buses, the grasses as far as the eye can see for the lawns of Stephen's Green on a summer's day, the crows for ducks, the cowshit for dogshit, the quiet for noise, the slowness for speed, the loneliness for no space to think *(Pause.)* Every single Friday, when I drive back down home, from college, I'm okay for the hour I am still in The Pale. I'm alright while the sky stays orange with the embers of a city. But the further and further inland I drive, the more my breath begins to shorten *(Pause.)* I'm just not made for it. I'm not cut for country living. Not their version of it. Not my version of their life *(Pause.)* There's a length

of time every evening when this farm
comes alive. And every morning. When
the cows are in, shouting and roaring at
each other and we're shouting and roaring
at them and for those few hours every day
I really feel like there's some hope, some
life, in this place. In every other hour, it's
silent. Still. I know every inch of this place
but I don't want it. I don't. I want to be
in a place where home is where I *am* and
not a three hour drive away every, single,
weekend. I want to feel normal, and know
what possibility means. I want to feel loved,
really loved, and love *him* back. I want
to trade farm for apartment block, cows
calving, hay-bailing and yard sweeping for
screaming babies on a bus, bursting Tesco
shopping bags on a busy street and messy
front gardens with too many flyers stuck in
front doors. I want so many people around
me their thoughts create noise. I want to
carve out a corner for myself in a city that
pretends you're not there but secretly needs
you. This is what I know about myself, this
is what I want. *(Pause.)* But you can't always
have what you want, and so you might as
well go back to focusing on whatever task
you have at hand.

3

BRENDAN: I schtep out of the milking parlour
before I hit one of the beasts a clatter.
They're fussed tonight. Unsettled. I put
on some aul music in the tape recorder
earlier, thinking it'd ease them but not
tonight. They're out for trouble tonight.
"Put on Freddie Pewter," roars the missus
at me, trying to stop a cow from kicking
at the tubes. Freddie Pewter. I'm killed
telling her it's Mercury. Freddie *Mercury*.
(Pause.) It's a fine evening. Dark, here in
the arsehole of winter, but fine. Thank
god. Crisp as you like. Beautiful, even.
The crows are up in the beech trees giving
out, like they always do. Making noise
and starting fights. Arrah. Let them at
it *(Pause.)* I can see my daughter, Jane,
standing in the yard looking up at the
trees. Holding an outside brush, still,
staring up at them crows. She should be
sweeping. I should be milking. But I'm
caught by the sight of her. Her shoulders
are hunched up, more than usual. I can't
see her face and I want her to turn and see
me and smile so I can leave and go back
to unsettled beasts. The look of her back,
her figure in the dark night, makes me feel
the cold. I'm not used to this, to seeing her

4

here, like this. Normally, she's gone back
to Dublin by this time. Like clockwork
every Sunday evening, into the car and
back to Dublin. Leaving me, and the wife,
and my eldest, Tim, around the farm. But
not this evening. She'll stay put because
that's what's best for her. Fresh air and
hard work, tire her out, so she can sleep
this off, this ...thing...that's come over her
(Pause.) "Normally." There's something
that's lost its meaning to me *(Pause.)* I
like having her around the farm but she's
just staring...she should focus on what
she's doing. "It's worse they're getting"
roars the missus from inside and it's
my cue to go back to what I know best.
Cows, milking, farming...land. I leave my
daughter alone in the dark, and go and
press play on the Freddie Pewter tape.

BOB: There's a queer air on the farm. Them,
all them, the Bossman, his wife, Tim, and
Janey, they all have a funny smell to them.
It unsettles me. And I don't like that.
Not one bit. I'm bouncing, happy out,
surprised to see my Janey but I don't like
the smell she's come home with *(Pause.)*
I heard Bossman and his wife talking,

snapping at each other last Sunday before they shoved Janey into the car and drove off, her blank eyes and fair skin staring out the window of the car as they passed me on the driveway *(Pause.)* They call me the *farm* dog but I'm not. I'm *her* dog. And when I saw her drive away like that, not knowing what was happening, I was a puppy again, scared, stupid, afraid of their uneasiness *(Pause.)* She was gone a week. Exactly. I know because it was Mass day when she left, and it's Mass day today. I know how it's Mass day because the bossman and his wife put on proper shoes and go off in the car together. I've never been to Mass but I've heard them talk about it and it sounds desperate boring. I waited and waited for Janey to show up, report for duty, as always, on Friday night. But, nothing. And yesterday, still no Janey, and no explanation. They weren't even talking about it. Then she arrived back today. With the mother *(Pause.)* Only the bossman went to Mass this morning. Herself had gone to get Janey from *wherever* she was all week. And that smell's been here since she got back this afternoon *(Pause.)* There's been a lot of

whispering *(Pause.)* The milking machines
are humming away and the beasts inside
the parlour are howling. Making noise
and causing upset. Maybe they can smell
it too. I sit by the door to the kitchen on
night duty. I should get up and go over to
the parlour for a sup of milk but tonight I
don't want to be near any of them. Which
is why I'm sitting here watching Jane
in the yard, and her father, over by the
milking shed, watching her. I wonder will
she tell me anything about where she was
all week. And will she tell me why she is
here on a Mass night and not in Dublin,
at college, or why the bossman is staring
at her so much, and then the smell blows
over from him and hits me straight in the
snout and the fur on the back of my neck
stands up as the smell becomes known to
me. It's everywhere in this night. I hunker
down and bury my snout deep below my
furry paws and snort outwards, pushing
it away, the heavy smell of human fear
rushing around me.

JANE: *(Monday morning.)* A wind has picked up
as I slosh my way through the yard and
over towards the top field. My eyes squint
in the mid-morning sun and I pull the

pink scarf around my neck tighter to keep out the cool air. The beginning of another week stretching out far in front of me turns the toast in my stomach. The crows in the trees grip tight their circus height homes on branches above. My wellies are too small for me and I can feel the nail on my big toe push back into my foot and I wince with every step.

BRENDAN: There was an, awkwardness, in the kitchen when Janey came down to breakfast this morning. Nobody mentioned where she'd been. What happened. What she was going to do. My wife put every piece of pork in the fridge in front of Janey, "you'll have a sausage...d'you want a rasher? G'wan, you'll have some pudding," talking incessantly, coping the only way she knows how, to feed the poor girl. We knew she'd best rest here for the week, help her get her, wits, back. I knew by the look of her that she'd been crying last night. I wanted her to leave all that up there in that *place*. That was the whole point of it. I wanted to wrap my arms around her and pull her in close. I wanted her to be six again, looking up to me like I was the only person in the world that mattered. I wanted to take away whatever it is that's hurting her, that I just don't understand. She sat down slowly into the rickety wooden chair she always sits in at our big kitchen table, pink scarf wrapped around her neck. "Are y'not too warm with that thing on," I wanted to say, but didn't. It was an effort for her to reach for a slice of toast and put it on her plate. She poured tea. It'd been there a while and she didn't seem to care. She liked good, strong tea. Always did. She's a fine country girl like that. I want nothing more than to have her here, on the farm but in my heart I *know* what she really wants, I *know* I should say to her, "pack your bags, you're going back to college" but something won't let me.

JANE: The muck on the ground beneath me squelches as I move, striding large towards the moving chaos in the middle distance. I can make out the cattle running around like headless chickens and as I get closer I can tell that my mother, father and brother are as bad as the cattle. Tim

yells at me to cut them off at the side
ditch and I make towards the gap but I
trip on a rock and go face down, my right
hand sliding splat through an old cow
pat, crusty on the outside, smushy on the
inside. I feel it going up under my nails,
and a shiver runs across my neck with the
sense of it. Picking myself up, I get back
to the task at hand. Lying on the grass in
the gap, the electric fence is down off its
stake. I lean down to pick it up and put
it back in its place. It takes a few seconds
but a slow pulse makes its way up through
my hands and into my arms, rushing into
a jolt. The wire is still live and I close
my eyes as I wrap my fingers around it
till my arms shake. For a moment, I am
escaped. I am away from here. I think of
Mark, and remember what it felt like to
kiss him. Of when he first put his hand
on my back and a jolt went up my spine.
How the hope and possibility of him and
me rose and fell so quickly. I squeeze
tighter on the wire, willing it to bring me
back to life. It feels sickly good for even
these few seconds and on the third shock
I drop the wire, stepping back from the
gap, quivering with pain, and adrenalin.

A vibration comes from behind me,
speeding across the top of the earth, and
hooves race past me, through the gap and
off into the next field, roaring for freedom.
My mother arrives first, shouting at me
but I ignore her, watching the cattle run
away, pleased for them. They'd gotten
one up on us. It doesn't happen to them
very often. I wonder would I be able
to escape like that, would I be able to
get one up on them. Dad comes tearing
towards us in the tractor with my brother
Tim in the front loader, who scowls at me,
seething with rage at my incompetence,
like I'd just ruined Christmas again. "You
might as well go home and make the tea if
that's how you're going to be," my mother
snaps at me as she trudges through the
gap towards the open field, focusing on
the galloping creatures ahead of her.

BRENDAN: Tim made a stupid mistake. He
didn't fix a gate and the cattle broke out,
which has me here, now, tearing around
the field like a buffoon. Grace, the wife,
is out of breath when she comes running
up the field and I can see where the sun
is turning her face older than her years. I

wonder does she resent this life we have? She has wrinkles all over her eyes and forehead from a lifetime of squinting in Irish country sun. The little of it we get. She'd a job in Dublin and moved back home when we married. She told me plenty over the years she was exactly where she wanted to be, but, I can't think of *why* a woman would want to work so hard in such tough conditions *(Pause.)* I can see Jane in the distance, walking through the muck at the entrance to the field. She has on that big pink scarf she loves so much and she's limping slightly. When she was a young girl, she used dress up in her mother's clothes, put on her high heels and shuffle around the house. One day, she put on my overalls and wellies and stumbled into the kitchen. The sight of this tiny thing, in pigtails, barely able to stay upright in my big old boots, it flattened me. I laughed so hard, she got upset, thought I was laughing at her, silly girl. I told her, "Daddy is laughing because Janey is the best thing since sliced bread." It was lost on her, and she took it fierce personal. After that, she wore her boots that bit too small, as a dig

12

against me *(Pause.)* I smile when I see it. Distracted by her *(Pause.)* Tim lets a roar out of him, and I turn back and focus on the task at hand. She isn't exactly hurrying to get to us. She's probably tired. No stamina, that girl has. Tim shouts at her to block the gap in the ditch. The electric fence is down and I know the beasts'll go tearing for it any moment. Jane makes her way towards the gap, and falls, face down. I hear Tim laughing but it's not funny. I wait for her to make a joke of it, a gesture, but she just picks herself up and keeps walking. Hooves tear through the field around us, going hell for leather, reeling in fear with their sudden freedom. I try to hoosh them back towards the farm yard but I can't take my eyes off Jane who's bending down now to pick up the fallen electric fence. I watch, confused, as she holds it in her hands, shock jolting into her pale, thin arms. Grace shouts at me to pay attention and I want to roar to Jane to turn around but I can't, I'm stuck stupid from seeing what she's doing to herself. The cattle race towards her and through her and off into the next field, followed by Grace trying to break a land speed record

to catch up with them. I hop into the
tractor and follow after.

JANE: I turn back towards home and make my
way down towards the yard. I think of my
mother, and her mountain of sausages,
and of the awkwardness my father had
made of breakfast, and wish he'd just open
his damn mouth and talk to me. About
something, about anything.

BRENDAN: I drive past my daughter as she
heads back to the house and I look and
look towards her but her eyes are dead
straight ahead, as if we didn't exist...
something is changing in her. I bounce
towards the gap, away from my daughter
and scan the top field for scattered, scared
beasts.

JANE: Bob comes trotting up to greet me and
as we walk towards the house, I notice
how badly parked my old car is by the
hedges in front of the barns. The red tip
of the corrugated iron roof on the hay
barn peeks up out of the damp yard. I
remember when Tim and I used to play
there for hours on end. Lost in our own

made up world. I remember when we used to roll around laughing on the hay. Make swing ropes. Build dens and castles and forts. I remember how happy I was in that red-roofed old barn.

BOB: I watch them make an arse of the cattle. I could go and help but I couldn't be bothered. Their mistake. They fix it. I'm angry at them for making Janey go out. She needs rest. A dog in the street can see that *(Pause.)* She comes back from the field very quickly and I walk back towards the house with her, glad of her company. She stops for a second by her old car, looking up at the top of the hay barn. I nudge her in the leg and she reaches down a hand to pet my head. Her hand has dung on it, I can smell it under her nails. I've just cleaned myself while watching them eejits race around the field, but I don't want to upset her by pulling away and so I let her rub my head and my soft ears and brace myself as I feel bits of it stick to my nicely cleaned fur coat. She goes inside, and I follow close on her heels, not waiting for an invitation. I stick right with her. She goes straight upstairs and into her bedroom and lies belly down on her bed, the way I do when I'm really tired, or when I find a warm spot on the ground. I stand in the doorway, unsure, as she drapes her arm down towards the floor and stares out into the small space of her room. The pink scarf on her neck gently cushions her face. Wruff! I bark, low, and soft, just to let her know I'm still there. "Come in", she says, and I trot in and sit by her bed and put my snout beside her face. I try hard to catch her attention, to nuzzle her, to make her smile but she just keeps staring, out, all blank, thinking things a dog knows nothing about. I don't like this. It makes me fierce uneasy *(Pause.)* When I can, I listen in to the bossman and his wife talk about her. I never got the chance to have puppies, they took care of that, and I don't like to talk about it. I've always seen Janey, like my own. She takes care of me, but I look out for her. They sit around and talk about what they think is best for her: let her drop out of college, spend more time on the farm, *work* it out of her system. Let the fresh air do her good. Do her *good*? It makes me growl at them, makes me

want to tear at their limbs and spit out
their flesh into the grey soil. I want to
bite their noses and bark in their ears till
they bleed. But I'm just a dog. I do that
and they'll take me out the back field,
lift and shotgun and put a bullet in my
head. And then Janey would be even
more alone *(Pause.)* I push my cold, wet
nose closer to her chin and touch it softly
to let her know I'm still here. A burning
sensation hurts the cold wetness of my
snout as I touch her dry, warm skin. A
jolt of electricity shoots through her, into
me and as it does I see them come. Fast,
heavy, bulking, laced with salt, and with
that fear that is everywhere since she
came home yesterday. Tears roll, one
after another out the corners of her eyes.
Some go to the sides of her nose and
into her mouth and some drop onto the
duvet cover and pink scarf beneath her.
I open my mouth slowly and softly put
my teeth to her hand, playfully, gently,
anything to distract her, help her. I feel
my slobber slide onto her small hand and
slick down her fingers and drop onto the
carpet below. I lick her hand, desperate
to pull her back from where she is going.

I sit, and nuzzle, and lick, and whine for
her to sit up and smile, but nothing I can
do is going to make that happen. I'm just
a dog *(Beat.)* What can I do to make a
difference?

JANE *(Friday night.)*: My week at home has gone
as expected. Dragging, long, punctuated
by...nothing. Normally I'm coming home
by now, not already here. I don't feel
today as any different to any other day
that's come and gone in its own time
(Pause.) What was the *point* of it all? To
put my family through that, and for what?
(Pause.) Their unease, their awkwardness,
their... shame, of me, is *excruciating (Pause.)*
I'm washing out the milking parlour with
the power hose, enjoying, even relishing,
the whoosh of the water as it beats clean
the bars and walls covered in cow shit.
I'm staying out of college till I need to. I
just want to sit still for a while. Be in one
place...but not here. There's no sitting still
here. Always something to do, cows to
milk, responsibilities, fences to fix, duties,
shit to shovel. They aren't saying anything
to me. They seem to be just, gliding along,
hoping I won't want to talk about it with
them. I wonder if I never say anything

and stay put, would they ever even ask
why I'm still here and not going back to
college in Dublin? This is the stuff of my
family, we keep schtum and don't talk
about anything. Like why Tim can't leave
the farm. He says he loves it, he works
hard, but he never gave over bitching
about it when he was younger. When he
went to college to study agriculture, he
dropped out like a hot snot. Came running
back with his tail between his legs. It was
too much for him. Too different for him.
When you live every waking moment
in the country, you live and breathe by
a different set of rules that don't apply
in other places like cities, or big towns.
And Tim was bred for one thing only:
land. *(Pause, she shrugs.)* Arrah, after the
age of fifteen, Tim stopped talking to me
about anything real. Just farm talk, or him
shouting orders at me *(Pause.)* Bob begins
to bark in the yard. He can hear a car at
the end of our laneway, making its way up
the windy road to our place. I go outside
to see the owner of the car, the bringer of
an event to this winter evening. An old,
blue Ford Fiesta revs to a stop close to
my car. It sounds like the exhaust needs

a bandage. I squint in the headlights, struggling to see who it is and suddenly I feel weak as the blood drains from my face as I watch Mark, *thee* Mark, the boy I think I like, get out of his car and look around. I dash back into the parlour to escape being seen but it's too late, Tim has spotted him from the hay barn and happily, chattily points Mark over towards me. Bastard. I scramble to rub clean the tiny bit of broken mirror on the grimy wall inside the parlour, desperate to see what sort of a state I'm in. My heart is racing as I pull off my filthy overalls to reveal an even less attractive outfit underneath. Dad's ziggidy Christmas jumper circa 1985 with holes in it with a pair of tracksuit bottoms that should've been binned years ago. And wellies that don't quite fit right with mans woolly socks peeping out over the top. Gorgeous. "There you are," he smiles at me. Here I am, I think, covered in cow shit and not really sure why you're here I am! He moves to kiss me on the cheek and I awkwardly step aside and our noses hit. He laughs as I go puce and curse my pale skin for its lousy blood vessels making me look like a tomato. The messy hair speckled with cow poo isn't helping either. Strands of loose hair standing on end, wild with neglect. We walk out into the yard and towards the garden where we can sit, in some privacy and I am only too aware of how I smell and purposely stride a good two feet from him. "'I've smelt cow shite before y'know," he laughs and my face shoots puce again. We walk through the rose-covered archway into the garden and I begin to feel a bit calmer. The garden is a haven amongst barns and sheds littered with clutter, tools, beasts, muck, shit and god knows what else. We sit on a small bench my mother bought in B&Q in Dublin last time she went up to visit her sisters. It gives a little when we sit but seems willing to take two arses. There is a silence between us but I'm bursting I'm so happy to see him. That he came all this way to find *me*. I cringe as I remember the phone call when I told him we'd never work out, lying through my teeth, knowing I couldn't juggle my two lives, and a boyfriend on top of it all. Ashamed that I just couldn't handle it. He draws breath, and asks why I've been out of college so long and where I've been.

I'm too ashamed to tell him where I've been, what I've been through. He says "I got concerned and thought I'd come and see if you were okay." His words slam my heart against my chest. I tell him he could've rang but he shoots me a look that says shut up, so I do. I listen, embarassed as he says he didn't understand why I shot him down so quickly when we'd clearly really liked each other. I can see in his eyes that he's a little bit angry with me. I try to lie to him about there being no real connection between us but he tells me I'm lying, and he's right, I *am* lying. Something about him, something about this big bulk of a guy, with his brown hair and browner eyes, seems to get in under my skin. He puts his hand on mine and I feel his clammy palms press against my knuckles and I realise that this is the first bit of affection or human touch I have felt since the last time we were together. The only time we were together. A wave of tears come flooding through me and I fight hard to keep it back but it flows, and flows, through me and around me. I press my head deep into the nape of his neck and weep for comfort and warmth. Mark

slides his big arms around my shoulders,
and squeezes tight, and I can feel my ribs
getting pressed together uncomfortably
but I don't budge because I want him to
hold me like that and not ever let me go.
In that moment, I am safe. I am okay.
Like I'm really worth something in this life
(Pause.) I've stopped crying a long time
when he finally lets go of me. I sit back
on the bench and realise the late dusk has
turned to night. He leans in and kisses me
and I kiss him back. His lips are soft and
I feel my stomach relax as I pull away.
He asks me to come back to Dublin with
him. I shake my head no, afraid of I don't
know what. He makes me *swear* to come
back up to the city by next week and as
words of promise bounce from my mouth
I realise that I believe them. In a second, I
feel belief, I am hope. I see his face smiling
warmly at me in the small light the moon
will give us, till dark clouds shuffle across
the sky and cover over the stars. I walk
Mark to his car and watch him drive away.
The crows sway and caw in the massive
trees high above us and Bob, sitting close
by my feet, barks at them to shut up. I feel
my heart empty out its contents as I turn

and walk back towards the house, wishing
I was in his car, driving away into the now
moonless night.

BRENDAN: Tim comes sauntering into the
house with a big smug smile on his face,
delighted with himself. 'Janey has a
gentleman caller,' he says to me. 'And
she's covered in shite.' He takes great
pleasure in knowing his sister has been
caught off-guard, unawares by her chap
dropping in unannounced. I feel like
giving him a belt but the last time I did
that we got into an awful fight and the
missus was crying and I hurt my arm. I
forget too easily how strong that boy is
(Pause.) Tim resents his sister. He couldn't
do what she does. Couldn't be away
from the farm. And she can. He's fierce
competitive. He gets it from his mother of
course. *(Pause.)* Tim moves on, whistling
his way out of the kitchen, delighted with
the bit of drama. I'm waiting for the kettle
to boil and Janey walks in. Tim was right,
she *is* covered in shite. Suddenly I see my
little girl again, before growing up took
hold of her. "Well," I say to her. Meaning,
who is he? Why did he call to see you?

24

Is he your boyfriend? Where's he from? Questions bursting in my head that I'll never ask her. She gives me nothing more than a shrug in response and stops at the kettle as it clicks to a boil, and wets the tea. I watch her pour two mugs, drop milk into her own, pick up her tea, and leave the kitchen as silently as she came in. Steam rises from my cracked old cup from Italia '90, and I feel my heart sink as I try to remember the last time I had a proper conversation with my only daughter.

BOB: I was born in a ditch two miles from the farm and was the only one to survive of my litter of three puppies. My brother got hit by a car when he was only two months and my sister got sick and died young, beside me in the ditch. I dragged her away and covered her in leaves with my puppy paws. My mother had left me, gone back to her own farm and I was trying to fend for myself. Jane was out walking with Tim, exploring, and he'd gone to the top end of the ditch I was hiding in. She was exploring where I was and my fur stood on end with fear when I heard her footsteps coming towards me.

I'd been fighting off big rats and birds
with my small baby teeth but I was weak
from no food and it was so cold at night
I wasn't able to fight anymore. I fell back
on my hind legs as the face of a twelve-
year old girl came at me through the copse
and pulled away a branch to look down at
me. She smiled at me. "Look at you," she
said. I thought she was an angel, that this
meant I was dead and going to a doggie
afterlife and when she reached in with
her right arm and lifted me by the scruff,
I thought that this was how all dogs go to
heaven *(Pause.)* "I found a puppy!" She
smelled like goodness, and lots of things
I had not yet smelled. I know them now
as fresh cut grass, daisies, baking bread,
lavender soap, farm air. She looked down
at me and stared into my eyes, serious
like, "I'm going to mind you puppy,
don't you worry." I closed my eyes and
softened to her warmth and I dozed,
finally, resting, as she bounced through
the fields, carrying me to her home. The
farm cats were none too pleased with my
arrival and it took a good few weeks to
build up my strength and show them who
was boss around the farm. They'd hiss at

me, sneer at me, "stupid dog," they'd say.
"Stupid, SMELLY, ditch doggie," and
go back to lying around doing nothing
useful. I learned fast to earn my keep and
worked hard to keep the bossman happy
(Pause.) At first, Janey would only let me
into the house when everyone was gone
away, or in to town, or at mass, or at the
mart. We'd sit and watch the telly machine
together, her on the couch, me on the floor
cleaning myself, watching her shows. And
she'd chat to me, tell me about school,
or a boy she liked. And I listened, happy
to be the one she talks to. When she was
sixteen, her parents started talking about
sending her to boarding school. It sounded
so far away and I know Janey liked the
idea of being away from the farm. Even
back then, she wanted to get away, do her
own thing. I couldn't bear a life without
her. She's my best friend, my angel, my
minder. Without her on the farm, I'd be
lost *(Pause.)* One day, we were lying on a
bail in the big hay barn. She was talking
to me, trying to make a big decision for a
sixteen year old. Boarding school, or not.
Leave home, or not. She was leaning back
on another bail of hay, focusing hard on

27

what to do. I was on the floor in front of her, my snout on her knee. *She* was talking to *me* but I was so upset at the thought of losing her that my ears started to ring and a bubble formed deep in my throat and worked it's way up until it was filling my mouth. My dog brown eyes stared straight at hers until the bubble in my mouth was bursting through my teeth and out onto my tongue it ran till a word came pouring out of me... '*Stay* '... *(Long pause.)* And she heard me.

JANE *(Saturday.)*: When I got back from the hospital last weekend, it felt like my worst day. I wanted to stay there. I didn't want to leave. Mammy talked the whole way home in the car and when she wasn't talking she had the radio on loud, blasting it so that even if I wanted to tell her how I felt, I couldn't. She was so desperate to drown out my thoughts, and went on and on about getting the hay barn fixed, that the hole in the roof was getting worse and Daddy would have to do something about it before Christmas comes. As houses and shops and traffic turned to fields and gates and wide open spaces, I felt my chest tighten. We passed the Dublin county

line and into County Kildare, travelling
South. The further and further inland
we drove, the more manic my mother
was talking. Her nervousness around me
was unbearable. She just couldn't accept
me. Like I was a huge failure to her, or a
dark secret. I knew she was lying to the
neighbours. There's no way in heaven
or hell she'd be telling them that their
daughter was in a mental institution for
a week to "settle her nerves" *(Pause.)* She
never *once* asked what was really going on
with me *(Pause.)* Down here, where I'm
from, they'll say, "there's Janey, she's a
depressive, don't you know." A depressive.
A depressive? It sounds like something
you'd use to flatten concrete. In Dublin,
they might say something like, "that Jane
young-one, she suffers terrible with her
nerves." Nerves? Me? "Desperate it is,"
they'd say. A depressive that suffers from
her nerves. They like if they can pigeon-
hole it, name it, pass it on to someone
else as the words come off their tongues
and on their next breath turn their heads
and gossip about someone else, who isn't
a depressive, about the state of the local
church after the vandals broke in, or

29

the bloody immigrants with no English
working in the Spar or how Imelda from
down the road got married on Saturday
and it did nothing only rain all day and
wasn't her dress absolutely disgusting but
sure are you surprised with all the bad luck
that's been all over that poor family for
years. They'll skirt, and dodge when they
don't want to talk about something but
anything else...oh boy, it's open season.
I sometimes wish so much I *was* Imelda
from down the road getting married
on a rainy day in a disgusting dress. I'd
rather be talked about like that, gossiped
about around town, than have my name
mentioned in hushed voices on street
corners in small towns, and have the words
"depressive" and "nerves" said about me as
if I'm contagious *(Pause.)* People just want
something to talk *about* but I just want to
have people *to talk to.* People who will look
at me and count me and not say "god isn't
it terrible she had to take them tablets at
such a young age" or "a hospital like that is
no place for a young girl." Or my personal
favourite, "but isn't she a gorgeous young
girl with everything going for her...what has
she got to be so upset about?"

BRENDAN: I'm trying to sleep, tired, from
another week of work but the missus is
tossing and turning since she got into
bed. There's only two things that keep
my wife awake at night. Tim, and Jane.
The two childer *(Pause.)* Janey stayed in
longer, *this* time. A full week. I thought it
would finally sort her out but the missus
told me she didn't utter one word the
whole way home in the car last weekend.
Kept staring out the window, she said, at
nothing. She probably couldn't get a word
in edgeways *(Pause.)* Grace is wide awake
at 2 am when I finally roll over and ask
her what's wrong. Her face is pure worry,
and the little line in between her eyebrows
on her forehead is even deeper than usual.
She's only looked like this a few times in
her life. Once, when her mother fell and
they thought she'd be in a wheelchair
and another time when Tim crashed the
car driving home drunk one night saved
only by Finnerty's side gate down the way
(Pause.) "I don't know about that doctor,"
she says to me, finally. "Janey's doctor.
I don't think he really knows what he's
about." As if she wanted me to pull his
medical certificate out from the drawer in

my bedside locker to prove that he was fit
to take care of our only daughter. I don't
know what to say. "What do you think
of him?" She asks me. I only met him
the once, that first time when we brought
Janey up to the hospital six months ago
for those few days. I didn't like the place.
Didn't like its fancy lawns and trees
and gardens pretending to be a hotel
when it isn't. I didn't like my daughter
being there. I didn't like that there
was something wrong with her *(Pause.)*
Wrong *(Pause.)* The doctor had corrected
me when I'd said there was something
"wrong" with Janey. He talked about
depression like it was a disease and I felt
a little clock begin to tick in my head. It
got louder and louder, telling me that if I
didn't get out of that room something was
going to explode inside my head. This was
not a place for my daughter: a nut-house,
a crazy farm. Dress it up in soft carpets
and moody lighting but it's still a mental
hospital. I left the room and walked as
fast as I could to get to the outside and I
burst into the fresh air gasping for breath,
screaming inside my own head that this
was not a place for my family, I raised

us better than this *(Pause.)* I waited until Grace came out forty minutes later, bullin' for me. I didn't even go back in to say goodbye to Jane. My own daughter. The shame of my shame of her was crippling *(Long pause.)* My wife shifts in the bed again and I can see how grey her hair is going at the roots. "She's going to be fine," Grace says, deciding. But I can see the fear in her eyes. And I can see that Grace resents Jane for putting her, us, through this. "She's going to be fine, I know it, it'll pass," my wife speaks again, convinced, convincing, and rolls over onto her side. I listen as her breathing gets heavier and she begins to snore lightly. I lean back into my big pillow and think about Janey, about Grace, about Tim, and about how I'm going to have to fix that hole in the barn roof before winter really sets in.

BOB *(Sunday.)*: I woke this morning to the sound of the bossman, up a ladder, hammering away, cursing at the hole in the roof of the hay barn. He must've been at it as soon as there was enough light, and by the looks of things, he hasn't made much of an improvement. He was like a *bull* when he came back into the kitchen. He must've

given up on it and next thing I heard was
the missus at him to get ready. Then *on*
went the nice shoes which means only one
thing... mass day. I knew Janey didn't want
to go. They left the kitchen door open
and I listened in, wanting her to kick up a
stink, break all hell loose, demanding to
stay at home, but she gave in at the first
hurdle. "Fight," I barked, "fight." The
missus was insisting she go, and Janey just
sighed, and wrapped on her big pink scarf
which was as good as waving a white flag
of surrender *(Pause.)* I dreamt about her
last night, before Tim stumbled home late
and woke me up with the smell of drink
and greasy chips. About her life in Dublin,
a big city I'd never been to and would
never get to. Sometimes, I'd see it on the
news when the kitchen door was open
and the telly machine would be on. One
time, when I snook in with her, Janey was
looking at photographs on the computer
box at images of a living room with lots
of young people in it. Janey was in one
photo with a young man who had his arm
around her. He was the boy who came to
see her. He's the only boy who ever called
for her. In the dream, we went to Dublin

and into that living room with all those
people and she felt safe. Happy *(Pause.)*
She used bring home big thick books with
pictures of bodies and muscles and bones,
so I settled that she was studying some
sort of medicine, or human bodies, or big
dogs. The bossman and his wife seemed
happy about it, proud, and I always got
the feeling she was doing something they
approved of, something... important.

JANE: The pen in my hand swirls easily through
my fingers as I twist it right, left, left, right.
The pad on the bottom of the pen helps
my right fore-finger grip nicely to it as I
twitch with it to make the words come out.
The notebook is one from school that I
found at the bottom of a pile of magazines
in my room. I kept the glossies over the
years because I used to like to make
collages in scrapbooks. I'd give each one
a theme and watch as they'd come to life
as I'd cut and stick and melt everything
together to shape one big picture. I have a
drawer where I keep all these scrapbooks
and old diaries and notes from friends
in school and photographs of nights
out and bits and pieces from over the

years. A drawer full of memories, ideas, expressions, depressions, suppressions. Instead of writing on this piece of paper I want to go and open the drawer and pull everything out, and search through it, for some sort of clue as to who I am, who I used to be. But I don't move from the chair I'm sitting in by the big window in my room. I don't want to catch even a glimpse of what's hid inside that drawer. It will only remind me of the makings of a life. Right now I need to keep her steady and focus on the task at hand. The pen with the lovely grip silks out a blue font of words, punctuation and emotion, heartfelt, heartmeant *(Pause.)* The outpour brings memories. I am nine, driving in the back of Daddy's old Toyota to Galway. Just the two of us. I felt extra special because I got to go and Mammy and Tim had to stay home and mind the farm. Daddy was going to Galway to see his sister Angela who had just broken up with her husband. Daddy didn't want to go but I had heard him and Mammy arguing and her telling him he had to. I didn't understand it at the time and now when I think about it I know that my father took me as a buffer,

so he wouldn't have to deal with any
real emotion. Auntie Angela was quite a
hysteric, or so Daddy would say, and the
last thing he wanted to do was drive the
long drive to Galway and listen to her
cry for two days. But he went, because
he knew he had to. There was nothing
more than duty in his presence. From the
moment he turned up he was like a big,
awkward plank, standing around, useless,
occasionally asking his sister if she was
sure about the separation. I found out
years later that Angela's husband had gone
off with some young one called Georgina
that worked in Supermacs and gotten her
pregnant and decided to stand by her. But
Daddy thought that Angela and Uncle
Tommy should just pull together, pay the
girl some money to keep the child, and
stay together for the sake of their marriage.
It wasn't until I was at least eighteen that
I realised what an eejit my father can be
(Pause.) But he could have not gone to
Galway, he could have rested at home and
not bothered with his sister at all. That's
got to count for something *(Pause.)* So
when I find that the words on the page are

starting to take some sort of shape, I realise
that I'm writing my letter to Daddy.

BRENDAN: I snort myself awake in the same
chair I fall asleep in every night of
the week, at the same time, doing the
same thing. In my lap is a half chewed
pencil with an auld notebook and some
paperwork for the farm. Herself is on
the phone and I can tell by the muffled
rhythms of her tones and pitches that
she is gossiping about something. Tim
is upstairs, on the computer, doing god
knows what. And Janey is taking a rest.
On the small nest of tables beside my
chair are a stack of glossy brochures of
sun holidays I don't want to look at but
I know herself will go on about it until
I do. I'm thinking that this time I will
tell her to bring her mother instead of
me. Maybe. I've never suggested this to
her before, I've just gone along on the
holiday and made the most of it. I'm not
ungrateful for a holiday, I've enjoyed
most of them but I've just kind of lost the
point in them. All that money to sit in the
sun under an umbrella or I'll end up like
a roasted turkey. Watered down drinks in

bars I can't speak the language of. Meeting
people, couples, our age and having
to pretend like we're new best friends
because we happened to come to same
place on holiday together. No thank you.
And then there's the time alone together.
I love my wife, I do, but our romance is
over. We're a bit long in the tooth for any
of that. And she knows it too. So all that
sitting alone together at every meal with
no farm or work to distract the big hole
of a conversation... it's too much work
(Pause.) One night, we sat in a restaurant
on a pier, in Lanzarote I think it was. I
could hear the mast bells and flagpoles of
boats banging together from the harbour.
It was a quiet enough place, a few around
us for their dinner. We said nothing for
twenty minutes. Just sat there. Not saying
anything. We're comfortable together.
We've gotten everything out there, over
the years, talked about everything. She
lifted her wine and took a sip and I looked
at her, with her pink sunburnt face and
she smiled at me and right there and then
I realised I have absolutely nothing left to
say to my wife *(Pause.)* And so I'd rather
she'd just go away on holiday with her

mother and enjoy it. Go round the shops, meet other people, chat to them, gossip, have a few drinks, get a bit tipsy, dance a little in the hotel bar to some terrible band that sings songs phonetically. No thank you *(Pause.)* The brochure on the top of the pile is a glitzy looking one for South Africa and I know immediately that it's going to be a difficult conversation if I say I won't go. I put my paperwork on top of a picture of Table Mountain and some young one in a bikini and stretch my tired arms upwards, feeling my back muscles strain with my reach. I move my head to one side, stretching my neck and look at the family photos on top of the dusty piano *(Pause.)* Janey is staring back at me in one of them. She's no more than six in the photo, big mop of blonde hair on her, and a big cheeky smile on her face. She's in a yellow dinghy and I'm pulling her along by a rope, wading through small, shallow waves, on a beach, somewhere in Spain. I get up and walk closer to inspect the photo and as I examine my daughter, my young, sweet daughter, I'm deafened by a voice in my head. "Fuck it, take them to South Africa, take the kids, your wife and your mother-in-law and everything will be okay in the family...*she'll* be alright."

BOB: The days are getting shorter for sure.
I've never been easily spooked but these
winter nights come so early and last
so long sometimes that I think they'll
never end. I can sense the shortest day
is only around the corner. Then it'll be
Christmas, and maybe things will change.
For a while, anyway *(Pause.)* Years ago,
was the only time the bossman's rubbed
my head, just the once, when I was a
puppy, and Jane had put a red ribbon on
my neck and he'd had another whisky.
He patted my head, and said, "Happy
Christmas dog." I think maybe he puts
up with me because of Janey *(Pause.)* He
never shows it, but, I think he'd do just
about anything for *her.*

JANE: It's the quietest time of the evening when
I slip down from my bedroom and into
the empty kitchen. On my chair by the
kitchen table hangs my beloved pink
scarf. I hesitate for a moment, knowing
how cold it will be outside. I reach to
take it, but my hand drops short and my

41

legs carry me out into the yard without it. I hear twigs breaking and falling to the hard ground beneath. Up till now, we've had a mild December but it turned yesterday and the air must be blowing in from the North because my nose tingles like it always does when it's cold. The cold makes me think of Mark. Winter started to wake up the night we went out. He had wrapped his arms around me as we walked around Stephen's Green. "I'm going to kiss you before we get to that next corner," he said. Oh my heart. Jumped in my chest with nerves, butterflies, lust. Love? *(Pause.)* I look at the driveway down towards the road below, and see him again driving off into the night without me beside him in the car. I think of the promise I made him, that I'll never keep. The hole where hope used sit inside me, widens.

BOB: I'm nodding off, into a delicious doze, when the kitchen door opens and Janey sneaks out. It's her house, her home, and I've not seen her sneak like this since she would play hide and seek with Tim when they were children. She slips her feet not

into her own, too tight welly boots, but
into her father's big size thirteens and
slouches out into the cold night of the yard.

JANE: My neck is cold. I miss my scarf.

BOB: The trees have been making noise all
night with their creeking and I'm spooked
by the sounds, the noises, their warnings,
their forebodings. I follow her towards the
barn, sniffing where her feet have made
marks on the damp ground from dragging
her too-big boots. I don't understand why
now, all of sudden, she's stopped wearing
the boots that are too small for her and
put on her father's big ones.

JANE: Bob's paws trot up behind me, curious
to see me, be beside me, happy of some
company on such an unfriendly night. I
tug at the rusting bolt on the barn door
and it slides across, swinging open.

BOB: I can smell something on her as I brush by
in front of her into the big silent dome. I
want her to go back inside and get warm
and stay away from a dark place like the
barn. It scares me and I wag my tail faster
to muster up some energy into the dead air.

43

JANE: The bare concrete ground of the yard outside takes on dust, hay and straw. I reach my right hand over and feel on the wall for the light switch and click it on beaming instant light into the barn. A softness looks back at me. The bailed hay sits neatly piled, cushioning any noise or sound underfoot.

BOB: I'm relieved when light beams in the big old place. I stay close to her but I can smell fear dripping down the walls of the space around her. She reaches down and pats me on the head and takes hold gently of my left ear and strokes its velvet softness with her kind hand and I feel how cold her fingers are, how much she's trembling.

JANE: I can barely look at him, his kind, soft doggie eyes radiating unconditional love and warmth into the space around us. His wagging tail breaks my heart and a deep freeze surges up inside my body, taking over my organs, my skin, my hair, my thoughts, my feelings, my memories, my everything, freezing up.

BOB: I jump on her but she pushes my paws
down as her whole body cools to a
freeze and I don't know what to do. My
senses are so confused, humans shouldn't
have this smell, this air about them and
I haven't ever seen it on one of them
before, least of all my lovely Janey.

JANE: Everything speeds up, on fast forward,
reminding me of all I have been, have
not been. But the freeze continues and
as soon as my brain wanders down a
laneway towards a memory, a thought,
I am cold to it, I am icy, I am steel, I
am determined. I am losing my self to a
power greater than me but I do what I
was always taught to do and focus on the
task at hand.

BRENDAN: The decision to go on a family
holiday makes me want to shout the
house down. With all the doctor visits,
the hospital stays, the trouble with
Janey, I know that this holiday will take
everyone's mind off things. I think about
how excited Grace will be when I tell
her my decision. I know Tim will shrug
his shoulders and give out about farm

relief but he'll be happy and won't show it. I know that Janey will be out and out excited. She once talked about going to South Africa, a few years ago but I told her they had malaria there and not to be thinking about it and she never mentioned it again but I know in my heart that she'll be over the moon when I tell her we're going. Malaria bedamned *(Pause.)* I want to tell her first, so she can feel special. The door to her bedroom is open a small bit and I knock as I walk in, forgetting to give her privacy in my excitement. The room is empty, which surprises me because she said she was going to take a rest. I figure she's in the bathroom and sit on her bed and wait for her. A minute goes by and I scan the room, looking at my daughter's things. Her trinkets, her details, her life, her bits and pieces. A pile of worn and clean clothes sitting on a chair waiting to be put away. Her shoes pulled off without undoing the laces. Beside her bed is a set of rosary beads her grandmother gave her and I pick them up and put them to my nose. They smell like my daughter and I know in that minute that I've never thought about how my daughter smells

before. Sweet, gentle, innocent. Like the
lovely smell you get when we cut hay,
or when my wife makes apple tart and a
smell of goodness wafts through the air
from the kitchen. I replace the beads and
see for the first time, how I missed it, I
don't know, an envelope with my name
on it. I pick it up, confused, curious. The
envelope is white, and not sealed. I see
from the ink that it cannot have been
written all that long ago and my big
thumb smudges my own name on the
outside of the envelope a little. I pull out
the letter and feel that it is about two or
three pages in length. I open it, holding it
up to the light so I can read the words:
"I don't know how to begin this so I will
just write what I am feeling deep inside."

(Beat.)

JANE: I know where to find rope.

BOB: She stumbles in her father's boots as she
reaches around the back of a rusty, old
loader and unties a piece of rope from
its holding place. It's long and thick.
She holds it in her hands, pulling on it,
checking it.

47

BRENDAN: My hands stiffen rigid and throw
down the letter, dropping the pages to
the floor and my legs heave my body
towards the door and out of her room.
Downstairs, I run, instinct carrying me to
the kitchen. I see her pink scarf, hanging
on the chair, panicking at the sight of its
bright colour. I rush to the dining room.
Then back upstairs to the bathroom. I
dash, like a wild animal, searching for its
lost offspring.

JANE: Climbing up on the bails of hay, I work
my way towards a strong supporting beam
running across the barn from side to side.

BOB: What sort of game are we going to play?
And why here? Why now?

JANE: For a moment I consider a position that
will leave me face away from the door but
my hands are tying a knot and there is
simply no time.

BRENDAN: My senses melt into one big
emergency to find my daughter and I rush
through the kitchen again and open the
back door to the yard. Cold air blows at me

and I look down at Bob's empty blanket.
My boots are gone. I slip into Tim's and
rush into the front yard, panic, fear, rises in
me, I see her car sitting idle, empty.

BOB: I let out a quiet whimper, enough to tell
her I'm here and I think we should leave.

BRENDAN: I search in the darkness, my eyes
adjusting to the night and I see light
shining out from that hole in the roof of
the hay barn and hear an old dog's voice
in the wind.

BOB: I yowl louder, I want her to come down
but she ignores me. I heave at my hind
legs, willing them to get up onto the hay.

JANE: Bob stares at me, screaming with his eyes
for me to come down from atop the hay. I
swing the rope around the beam, catching
it first time, and slowly, surely, I hoist the
rope around my neck.

BRENDAN: I reach the barn door and put my
right hand onto the big bolt –

JANE: – I think of nothing but the task at hand –

BRENDAN: – A shot of ice races into my skin and burns my bones in my fingers –

BOB: – I fight and fight but my old legs cannot get up to be with her –

JANE: – I look down at Bob –

BOB: – I'm howling now, LISTEN TO ME, HEAR ME, TALK TO ME –

BRENDAN: – I pull the steel bolt across, with every bit of strength I have –

JANE: – I lean out off the high stack of hay and I hear him tell me something –

BOB: – She turns, and she stares down at me, *her* eyes into *mine* –

BRENDAN: – Where are you? Jane? Where are you? –

JANE: – A word comes from him –

BOB: – "STAY" –

JANE: – but it's too late –

BRENDAN: – I heave the metal door open –

BOB: – She blinks, looks away, and steps out –

JANE: – And then I am gone, lost to the world I can no longer bear.

(Beat.)

BRENDAN: The depths of hell drag my heart from its place and murder me in my standing-

BOB: – Her father's boots slip from her small feet as they lose their grip and fall crashing to the floor, leaving her limp body for the last time –

BRENDAN: – Breath, leaves my body and I fall back into the barn door but it spits me forward, pushes me towards the hay –

BOB: – Tears flood into my eyes and I cry, I bark, I snarl, I spit, venom racing through my teeth –

BRENDAN: – I scramble desperately, roaring every sound that my body will make –

BOB: – I cannot make enough noise –

BRENDAN: – Clawing at hay bails, with my bare
hands –

BOB: – In this god-forsaken barn –

BRENDAN: – For height, for strength, for
saviour, for life.

(There is a long pause.)

BOB: I fall to squat, sinking down on all
fours, my two front paws touching the
wellington boots, lying empty,on the soft
floor beneath her.

(Long pause. Lights come fully up.)

JANE: The beech trees in the yard on our farm
are tall. So big, they sometimes feel like
they block out the sky.

*(Lights rise to such brightness the whole theatre and audience lights
up. Then, blackout.)*

THE END

By the same author

This Beautiful Village
9781786828293

WWW.OBERONBOOKS.COM

Follow us on Twitter @oberonbooks
& Facebook @OberonBooksLondon